· THE WAY THINGS WORK ·

BUILD YOUR OWN GUILLOTINE

· MAKE A MODEL THAT ACTUALLY WORKS ·

EDMUND V. GILLON, JR.

A Perigee Book

Perigee Books
are published by
G. P. Putnam's Sons
200 Madison Avenue
New York, New York 10016

ISBN 0-399-50620-9

First Perigee printing, 1982

PRINTED IN THE UNITED STATES OF AMERICA

INTRODUCTION

The guillotine, history's most dreaded and infamous instrument of decapitation, is most popularly associated with its use in France during the Revolution. In its most common construction, it consists of two upright posts surmounted by a crossbeam, and is grooved so as to guide an oblique-edged knife, the back of which is heavily weighted to make it fall swiftly and with force when the cord by which it is held aloft is let go. It takes its name from Dr. Guillotin, a noted humanitarian who advanced its use in France on the grounds that it caused death quickly and painlessly. In the spirit of the new Republic, Dr. Guillotin, who was elected to the Constituent Assembly in 1789, argued for decapitation by machine regardless of social status. Previously the privilege of decapitation was confined to persons of noble birth. The machine he recommended, called the *mannaia,* had come to his attention in an article he had read describing an execution that took place in Milan in 1702.

The first detailed description of the machine in France was contained in a cost estimate presented to the National Assembly in 1792. It was called "La Petite Louison." After testing its effectiveness on live sheep and dead bodies from the hospital of Bicêtre, it was erected on the Place de la Grève in Paris and used for the execution of the highwayman Pelletier on April 25, 1792. For some time after its first use there was much debate among the medical community as to whether the head retained its faculty of thought and was able to see, hear, and smell after it was separated from the body. It was finally concluded, much to the relief of the humanitarians, that death was instantaneous and total.

The guillotine had been in use in Scotland, England, and various parts of the Continent for centuries before its introduction into France by Dr. Guillotin. In Edinburgh there is still preserved in the Antiquarian Museum a type of guillotine called "the Maiden," which was used to decapitate the regent Morton in 1581. In Germany the machine was called the "Diele," "Hobel," or "Dolabra" and was in general use during the Middle Ages. The German guillotine resembled a Chippendale highboy without legs. Italy employed the guillotine for the decapitation of criminals of noble birth from the thirteenth century to the beginning of the eighteenth. For about a century it fell into disuse on the Continent until its reintroduction by Dr. Guillotin. The guillotine was used in France until its abolition by the Mitterand administration. It is ironic that Dr. Guillotin, the humanitarian, has achieved immortality by his name being lent to a machine of such terrible reputation.

This model also includes a tumbrel, a typical farmer's tipcart, which, during the Revolution, became the standard vehicle for carrying condemned persons to (and from) the place of execution.

Recommended Reading

Guillotin 1738-1814: The Good Dr. Guillotin and his Strange Device, by André Soubiran (London: Souvenir Press, 1964).

Photograph courtesy of New York Public Library

GENERAL INSTRUCTIONS

WHAT YOU NEED TO BUILD A GUILLOTINE: An X-acto knife, glue, a metal-edged ruler or a draftsman's triangle, masking or cellophane tape. You will also need about ten hours' time. Relax! It's not as difficult as you may think.

TIPS BEFORE BEGINNING

READ THE INSTRUCTIONS COMPLETELY. Examine the keys to the symbols carefully. Don't make the mistake of cutting on a line that indicates a scored fold. The instruction symbols appear on several pages along with the pieces. This paper model employs post-and-beam construction. Thus it is important that before you assemble the pieces all the glue on the timbers be thoroughly dry to ensure that the timbers are sturdy enough to be inserted into one another.

SCORING: The pieces of this book require crisp, neat edges. To make a crease in the paper so that folds can be made sharply, use a ball-point pen or the dull edge of a scissors. If you use an X-acto knife for scoring, use a very light touch so that you don't cut through the paper (or use the dull edge). If you make a mistake and cut through a piece while scoring, the damage can be repaired from the back with cellophane tape. *Score exactly on the score marks indicated, and score each piece before cutting it out.*

CUTTING: Each piece should be removed as carefully as possible; cut away as much of the black line as you can. Also be sure to cut out all pieces marked with an X before you assemble them. It is too difficult to cut them out after the pieces are constructed. You will note in the instructions that there are several places where you should paste various pieces together *before* the larger piece to which they are attached is removed from the page. Follow these particular instructions carefully for the best results.

GLUING: A white glue that becomes transparent when dry, such as Elmer's or Sobo, is best. Use glue sparingly, but be sure to cover the entire surface of each tab so that the edges joined together stay together. Before you glue a piece in place, check the appropriate illustration; when gluing together wall pieces and shaft pieces check alignment carefully. Be sure to allow sufficient time for drying before handling.

ASSEMBLING INSTRUCTIONS

Right now, this book looks very much like a book. Ultimately, this book will look and work very much like a guillotine and tumbrel. The first thing you must do is to remove the staples holding the book together without tearing the sheets. Score each piece on each sheet before cutting except where the instructions tell you to cut a piece out first. Each piece is coded with a number and a letter; the letters follow the assembly order, the numbers indicate the pieces required for each section. Be careful not to cut the gluing tabs on each piece. Examine the drawings and read each step carefully before proceeding from one step to the next.

Step 1: Constructing the Scaffold Base

Begin building the scaffold by constructing the beams, posts and diagonal bracing beams A1, A2, A3, A4, A5, A6 and A7. (See the special note on the last page for the best method of constructing the timbers.) Insert the lower beam A2 into the openings near the bottoms of posts A1 and A3 so that the opening in the middle of beam A2 faces up. (See fig. 1.) Insert the middle post A4 into the opening in beam A2. Now lower beam A5 onto the tops of posts A1, A4 and A3 so that the posts fit into the three openings on the underside of A5. Glue the bracing beams A6 and A7 to the end of beam A2 and to the top of post A4 (fig. 1). Construct beams, posts and bracing beams A8, A9, A10, A11 and A12. Insert the middle post A9 into the opening of the lower beam A8. Lower beam A10 onto the top of post A9 so that the post fits into the opening on the underside of beam A10. Glue the bracing beams A11 and A12 to the ends of beam A8 and the top of post A9 as shown in fig. 1. Follow the same procedure for assembling pieces A13 through A19 as you used for constructing A1 through A7. To assemble pieces A20 through A24 use the same procedure that you used for constructing A8 through A12. Connect side A1 through A7 to side A8 through A12 by gluing the end of beam A8 to the bottom of post A3 and the end of beam A10 to the end of beam A5 as shown in fig. 1. Connect side A8 through A12 to side A13 through A19 by gluing the end of beam A8 to post A13 and the end of beam A10 to beam A17. Do *not* glue side A20 through A24 to complete the base yet.

Step 2: Constructing the Scaffold Floor

Construct beams A25, A26 and A27. Insert beams A25 and A26 into the two openings in beam A10. Now push beam A27 onto beams A25 and A26 so that the two beams A26 and A27 go all the way through the two holes on beam A27. Slide A27 forward until it is aligned with the tops of posts A4 and A16. Glue in place. When the glue is dry push the top beam (A22) of the side of the scaffold base not yet attached (A20 through A24) onto beams A26 and A25 so that they fit into the two openings in beam A22. Glue the end of beam A22 to the end of beam A17 and the end of beam A20 to the bottom of post A15. Now glue the other end of beam A22 to the end of beam A5 and the other end of A20 to the bottom of post A1 (figs. 1 and 2). Cut the red lines of floor section A28 while it is still on the page. Cut out strip A29. Turn over the whole page containing floor section A28 and glue A29 to the area indicated by the white strip. Turn over the page once again and carefully cut the outline of floor A28 to free it from the page. Dot glue along the tops of beams A5, A10, A17, A22, A25, A26, and A27. Lower floor A28 onto the beams (A5, A10, A17, A22, A25, A26, A27) so that the floor overhangs equally on all four sides of the scaffold base.

Step 3: Constructing the Stairs

Cut along red lines on pieces A30 and A39. Construct stair frame A30 and A39. Score and cut out stairs A31, A32, A33, A34, A35, A36, A37 and A38. Fold each step in half and glue it together so that each step has a double thickness. After the glue has dried thoroughly insert each step into the two stair frames A30 and A39. Glue the tops of stair frames A30 and A39 to the places indicated by the alignment marks on beam A10. (See fig. 1.)

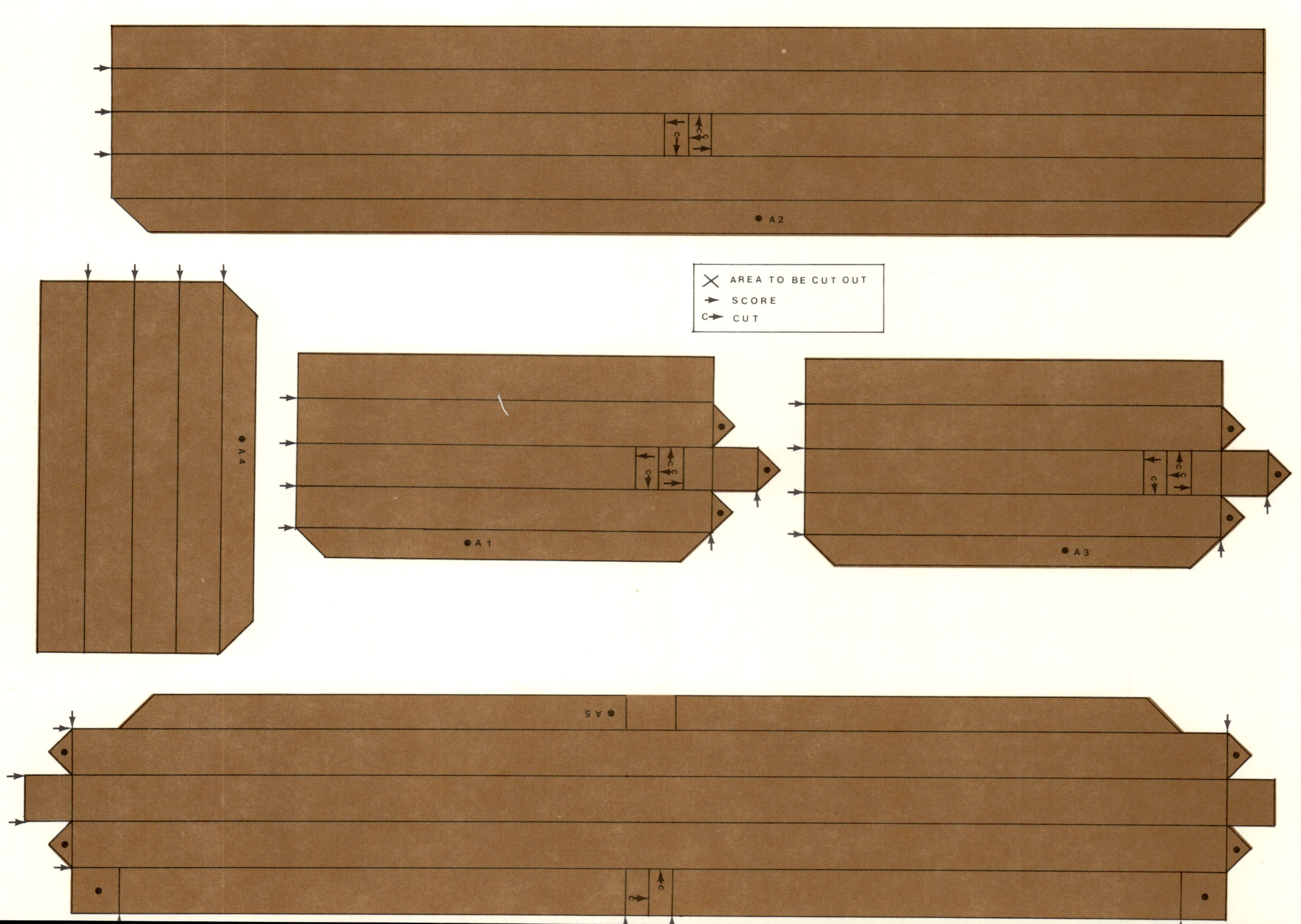

A 2
AREA TO BE CUT OUT
SCORE
CUT
A 4
A 1
A 3
A 5

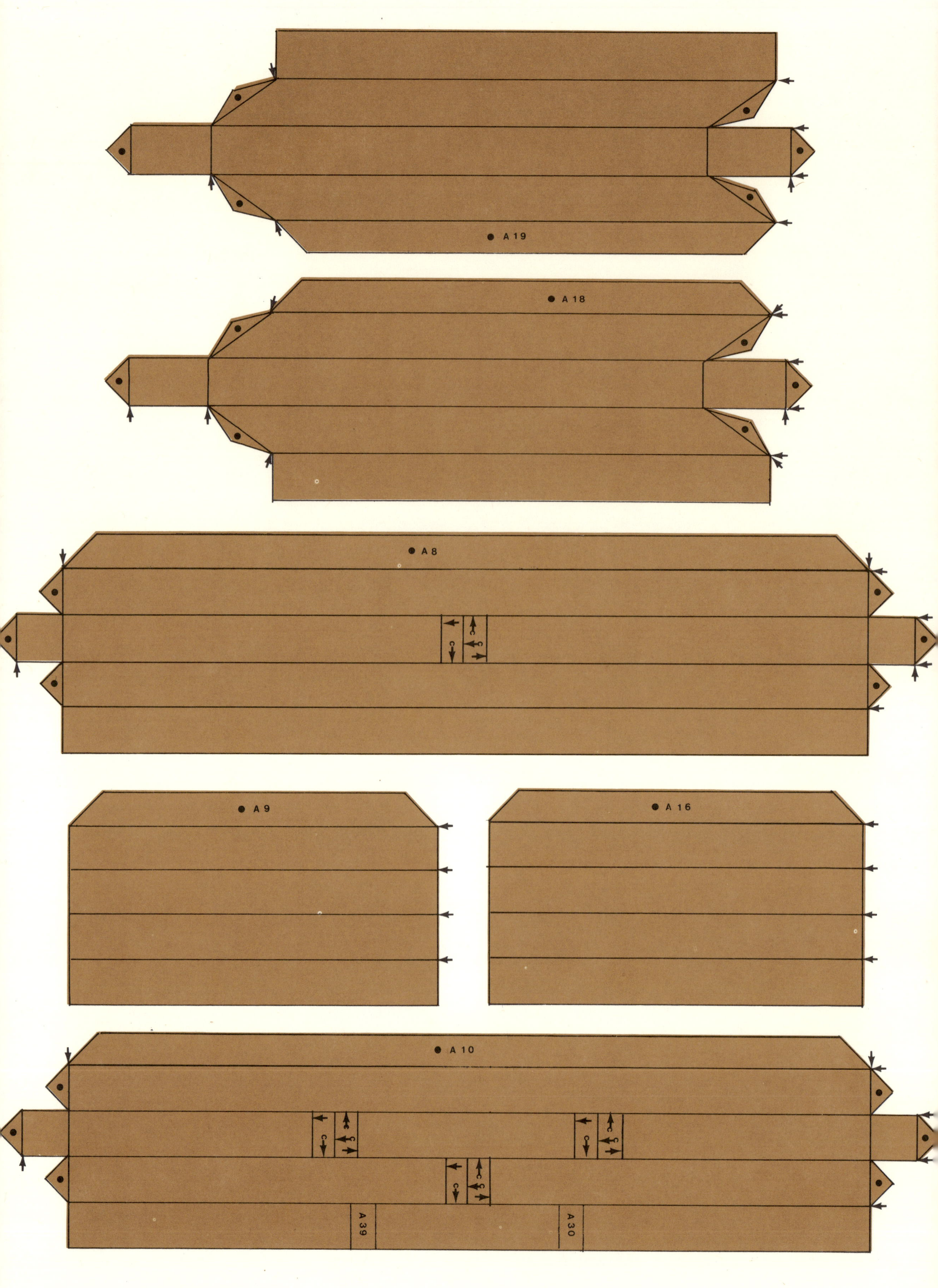

A 19
A 18
A 8
A 9
A 16
A 10
A 39
A 30

A 25
A 20
c
c
c
c
A 24
k
A 21

FIGURE 1

B 22
B 21
B 16
B19
B18
B20
B17
B 13 a
B13b
B 14
B 13
B 15
B 1
B 2
C 12
C 10
C 5
C 11
C 8
C 7
C6
C 9
C 5
C 2
C 4
C 3
C13
C14
B 7
B 8
B 31
B28
B 5
B 23
C 1
B 3a
B 6
B 29
B 27
B 30
B 4
B12
B 9
B 3
B10
B 11
B 26
B 25
A 28
B 24
A 1
A 27
A 25
A 29
A 5
A 26
A 6
A 10
A 4
A 12
A 9
A 2
A 7
A 11
A 8
D 4
D5
D 7
D8
D6
D 1
D2
D3
A 3
A 31
A 32
A 33
A 34
A 35
A 36
A 30
A 37
A 38
A 39

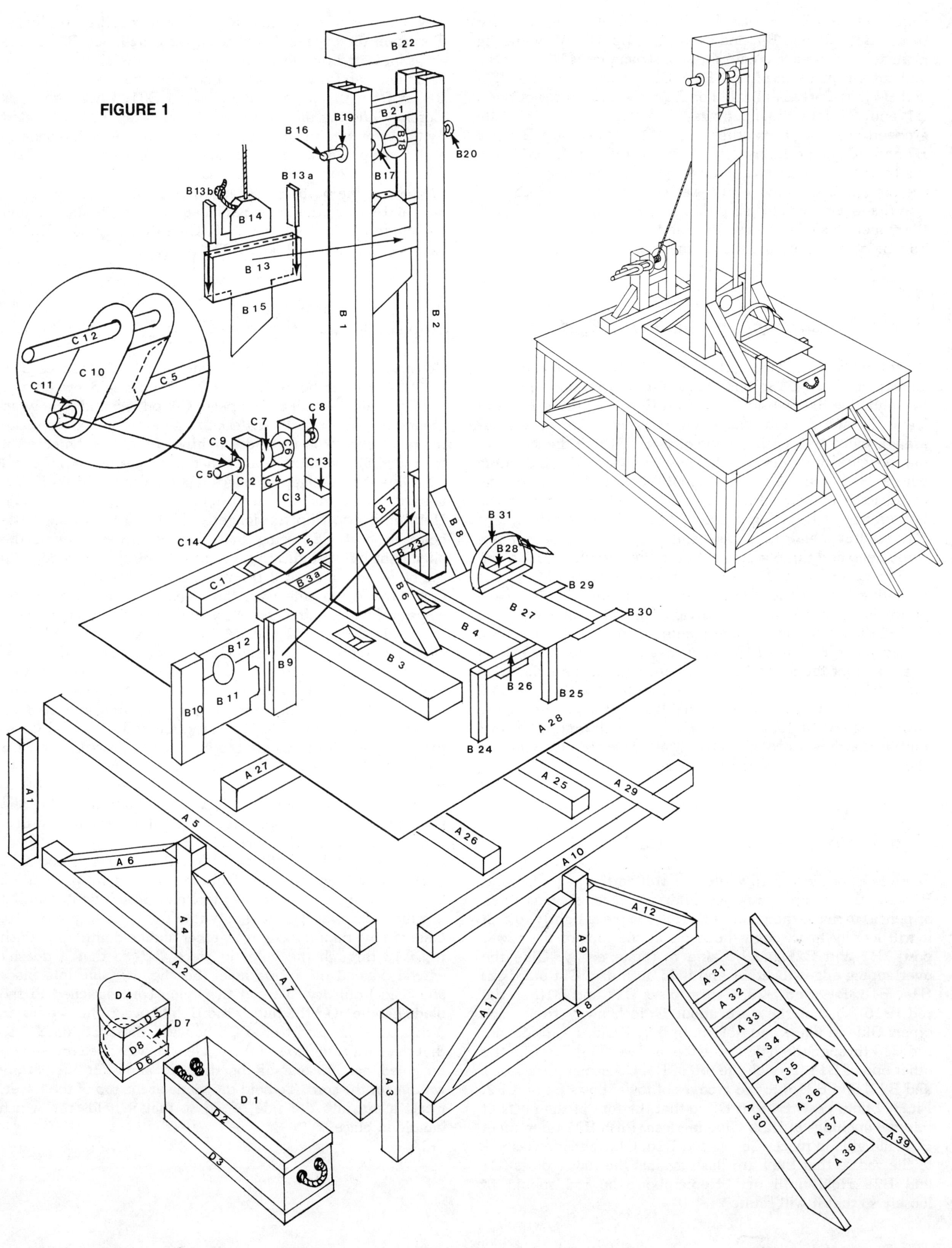

Step 4: Constructing Tower Posts

Construct grooved tower posts B1 and B2 (see fig. 1), base beams B3, B3a and B4, and braces B5, B6, B7. After cutting along the red lines to create slits, construct pieces B9 and B10 and cut out pieces B11 and B12. Glue base beams B3, B3a and B4 to the areas indicated on floor A28. Insert tower posts B1 and B2 into the openings of B3 and B4 so that the grooved sides face each other (see fig. 1). Glue braces B5, B6, B7 and B8 into positions shown in fig. 1. Insert piece B10 into the bottom of the groove in tower post B1 and piece B9 into the bottom of the groove in tower post B2. Insert piece B11 into the lower slits of pieces B10 and B9 and piece B12 into the upper slits of B10 and B9 (see fig. 1). Piece B12 should now be able to slide up and down.

Step 5: Constructing the Guillotine Blade

Score and cut out pieces B13, B13a, B13b, B14 and B15. Construct pieces B13a and B13b. Fold B15 along the score line and glue the two sides together. Construct piece B13 but leave top and bottom flaps open. Now glue the rectangular area of piece B15 to the inside of piece B13 on the side that has no glue tabs. (The rectangles on piece B13 indicating where B14 will be placed should be at the top of the constructed piece B13/B14. See fig. 1.) Close and glue the bottom flap of B13. Slip pieces B13a and B13b inside piece B13 so they stand up at both ends (fig. 1). Fit nine pennies three deep and three across between the end fillers B13a and B13b inside piece B13. (This is to give weight to the guillotine blade.) Close and glue the top flap of B13. Take approximately 16 inches of nylon cord. Tie one end and thread the other end through the underside of the scored and folded piece B14 until the knot meets the hole. Then knot again so that the second knot is flush against the hole. Glue piece B14 to the areas indicated on both sides of piece B13. Insert the completed blade and holder into the grooves of the tower posts B1 and B2 and allow it to slide down until it rests on the tops of posts B9 and B10. Make sure the blade falls on the side of the stocks opposite the stairs.

Step 6: Mounting the Pulley Rod

Score lines of piece B16 while it is still on the page. Cut out B16 and then wrap around a cylindrical object (such as a pen or pencil) to make the piece curl. Roll the piece tightly so that it will loosely fit through the holes at the tops of the tower posts (B1 and B2) and be able to rotate easily. Glue the overlapping edges together and hold until dry. Cut out disks B17, B18, B19 and B20. Center disks B17 and B18 on the rod (B16) so that they are about ¼ inch away from each other. Glue in place and hold until dry. From the inside slip rod B14 through the hole at the top of tower post B2. Slip the other end of B14 through the top of B1. Construct pieces B21 and B22. Slip B21 into the grooves of tower posts B1 and B2. Fit B22 onto posts B1 and B2 so that the tops of the posts fit into the openings of B22. Glue in place. Push B21 up to meet B22 and glue in place. Center rod B16. Glue outside washers to the rod so that they are flush against the tower posts (B1 and B2). Hold until dry. Remember—the rod should fit loosely so that it will rotate.

Step 7: Constructing the Body Shelf

Cut red lines of body shelf B27 while it is still on the page. Turn over the page and glue strips B28, B29, and B30 to the areas indicated by the white strips. Turn the page over once again and carefully cut the outline of the body shelf (B27) to free it from the page. Cut out strap B31. Curl both ends loosely. Glue the middle section of the strap B31 (indicated by the arrows) to the area indicated on B27. Attach buckle to end of strip. Construct posts B24 and B25 and beam B26. Glue beam B26 to posts B24 and B25 so that it is flush with the tops of the posts. (See fig. 1.) Glue the bottoms of posts B24 and B25 to the areas indicated on brace beams B3 and B4 and to the scaffold floor A28. Glue the body shelf B27 to the tops of beams B26 and B23.

Step 8: Constructing the Winch

Construct posts C2 and C3, beams C1 and C4, braces C13 and C14, and cut out disks C6, C7, C8 and C9. Score lines of rod C5 while it is still on the page. Cut out C5 and then wrap around a cylindrical object (such as a pen or pencil) to make the piece curl. Roll the piece tightly so that the diameter of the rod (C5) is slightly smaller than the holes in posts C2 and C3. Glue the overlapping edges together and hold until dry. Glue disks C6 and C7 to the alignment marks on rod C5. Hold until dry. Slip the longer end of rod C5 through the holes in post C2, going first through the side with the alignment marks indicating where C4 will be attached. Slip the other end of rod C2 through the holes in post C3, going first through the side with the alignment marks indicating where C4 will be attached. Now glue the ends of beam C4 to the inside of posts C2 and C4 on the areas indicated by the alignment marks. Glue beam C1 to the area indicated on floor A28. (See fig. 1.) Insert posts C2 and C3 into the two openings in C1. Glue brace C14 to the area indicated on beam C1 and to post C2. Then glue brace C13 to the area indicated on beam C1 and to post C3. Glue disks C8 and C9 to rod C5 so that they are flush against the outsides of posts C2 and C3 and so that the central disks are centered between the two posts. Hold until dry. Remember—the rod should be able to rotate easily. Construct piece C10 and cut out disk C11. Slip C10 onto the longer end of rod C5 until it rests against disk C9. Glue in place. Glue disk C11 onto rod C5 so that it rests against piece C10. Hold until dry. Score lines of rod C12 while it is still on the page. Cut out C12 and wrap around a cylindrical object to make the piece curl. Roll it tightly until it is a diameter that will fit snugly into the holes of piece C10. Glue the overlapping edges together and hold until dry. Push rod C12 through the holes in piece C10 so that it doesn't extend beyond the inside hole. (See fig. 1.) Glue into place and hold until dry. Thread the nylon cord attached to the blade handle over the pulley rod B16 between the two inside disks. Glue the cord to rod C5 between disks C6 and C7 so that the cord is taut when the blade is down. The cord should be glued next to one of the disks to allow for the lateral winding of the cord. To hold the blade at the top of the tower, insert a pin into the side of C2 so that it holds the winch handle in place.

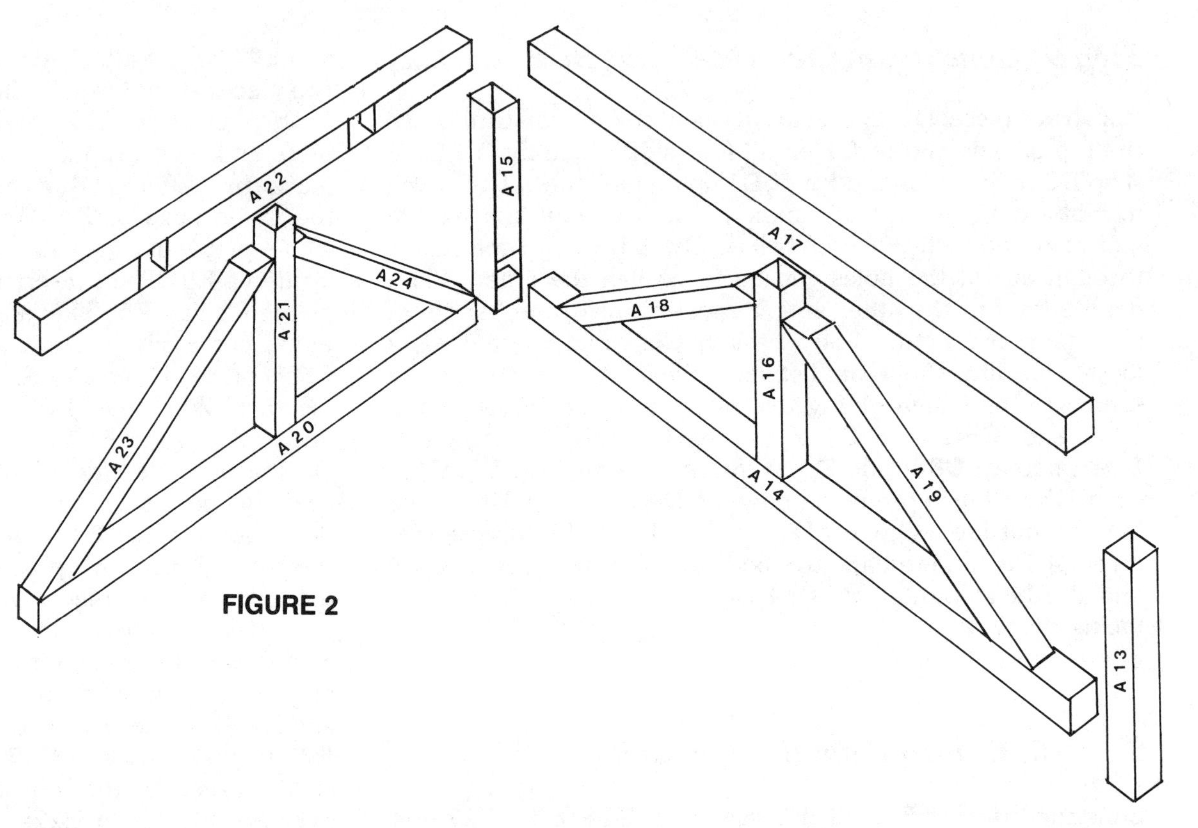

FIGURE 2

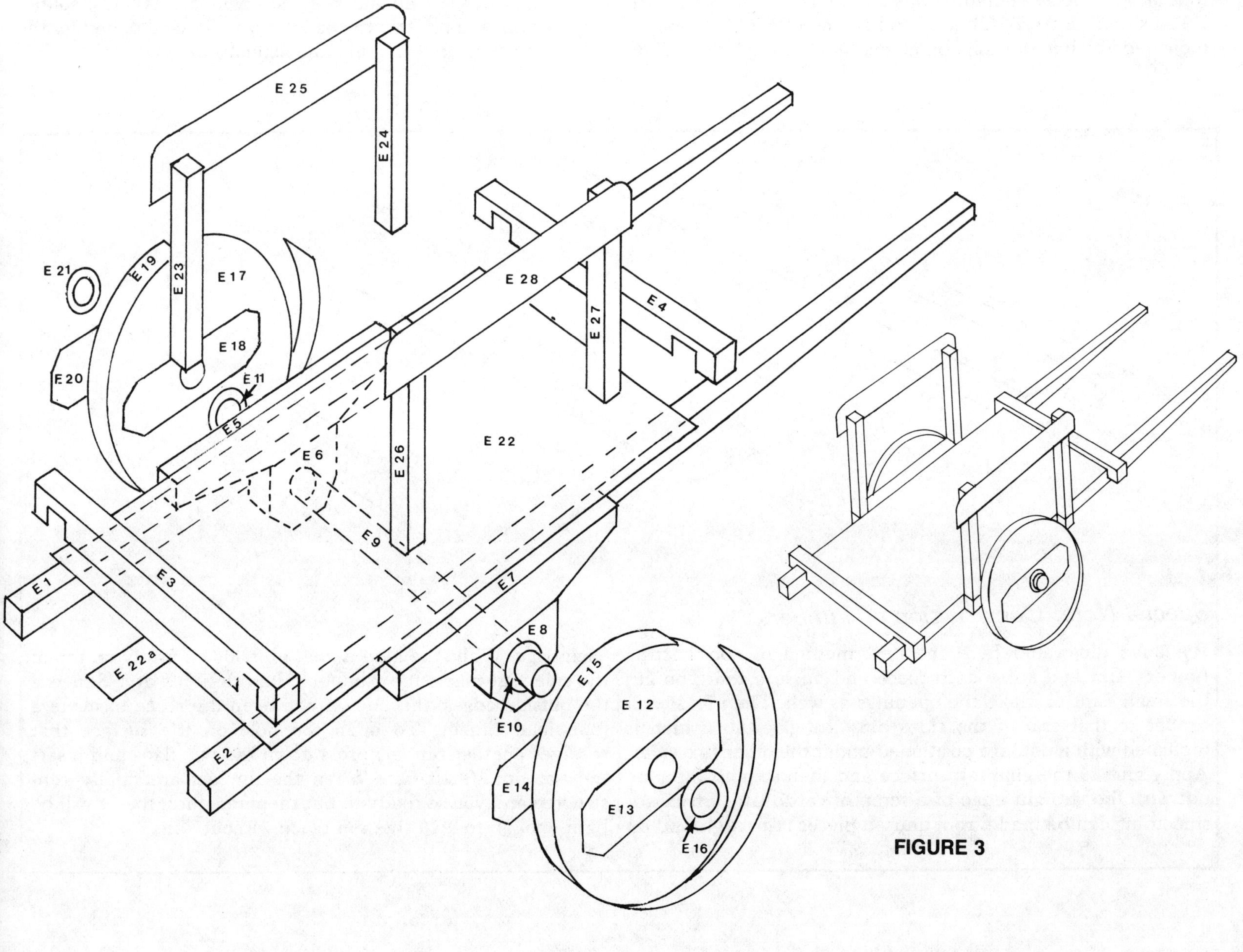

FIGURE 3

Step 9: Constructing the Head and Body Baskets

Construct piece D1 to create an open box. Glue strip D2 to the top outside rim of D1 on all four sides. (See fig. 1.) Glue strip D3 to the bottom edge of D1 on all four sides. Use twine to make handles for body basket. Tie a double knot in the end of a two-inch piece of twine. Thread it from the inside through one of the holes and back through the other. Tie a double knot in the other end. Repeat to make the handle at the other end of the body basket. Construct piece D4 by loosely curling the strip between the fold lines to form a semicircle and then gluing the glue-tab to the inside of the other end. Glue strip D7 to the inside bottom edge of D4. Insert bottom D8 inside D4 so that it rests on strip D7. Glue strip D5 to the top outside edge of D4 and strip D6 to the bottom outside edge of D4. Place the body basket (D1 through D3) underneath the body shelf (B27 through B30) and the head basket at the base of the stocks on the side facing the winch.

Step 10: Constructing the Tumbrel

Construct timbers E1, E2, E3, E4, E23, E24, E26, E27 and pieces E5, E6, E7 and E8. Fit timbers E1 and E2 into the notches of crossbeams E3 and E4 at the places indicated on E1 and E2. (See fig. 3.) Glue in place. Glue E5 to the side of E1 at the point indicated so that alignment marks showing where E23 and E24 will be attached are on the outside. The tops of both pieces should be flush. Glue E6 to the bottom of E5 as shown in fig. 3. Glue E7 to the side of E2 at the place indicated so that the alignment marks showing where E26 and E27 will be attached are on the outside. The tops of these two pieces should also be flush. Glue E8 to the bottom of E7. Score lines of axle E9 while it is still on the page. Cut out the piece and then wrap around a cylindrical object to make the piece curl. After scoring the glue strip, cut out and glue it to the inside edge of E9. When it is thoroughly dry, curl the whole piece and glue the other half of the glue strip to the inside of E9. Then insert the axle E9 through the holes in pieces E8 and E6. The axle should fit loosely in the holes so that it can easily rotate. Construct wheel E12 by folding the whole piece in half where indicated and gluing the two halves together. When the glue is thoroughly dry, cut along the red lines. Glue brace E13 to the places indicated on wheel E12. On the opposite side of E12 glue brace E14 to the corresponding position. Now cut out the wheel E12. Apply glue to the edge of wheel E12 and attach strip E15, centering it on the edge. Repeat this procedure to construct wheel E17 with the corresponding pieces. At each end of axle E9 place one of disks E10 and E11 and then wheels E12 and E17. Glue disks E16 and E21 to the ends of axle E9 and hold until dry. Glue posts E23, E24, E26 and E27 to the places indicated on E5 and E7. Glue piece E25 to the tops of posts E23 and E24 and E28 to posts E26 and E27 as shown in fig. 3. While it is still on the page, cut the red lines on piece E22. Turn the page over and glue strip E22a to the white area. Turn the page over once again and cut along the outline of E22 to free it from the page. Lower E22 onto frame E1 and E2 between beams E3 and E4 and glue into place.

And now, you're all finished! Strap in a small toy soldier (you'll have to remove the head), turn the handle, and let the blade fall. See how a guillotine actually works.

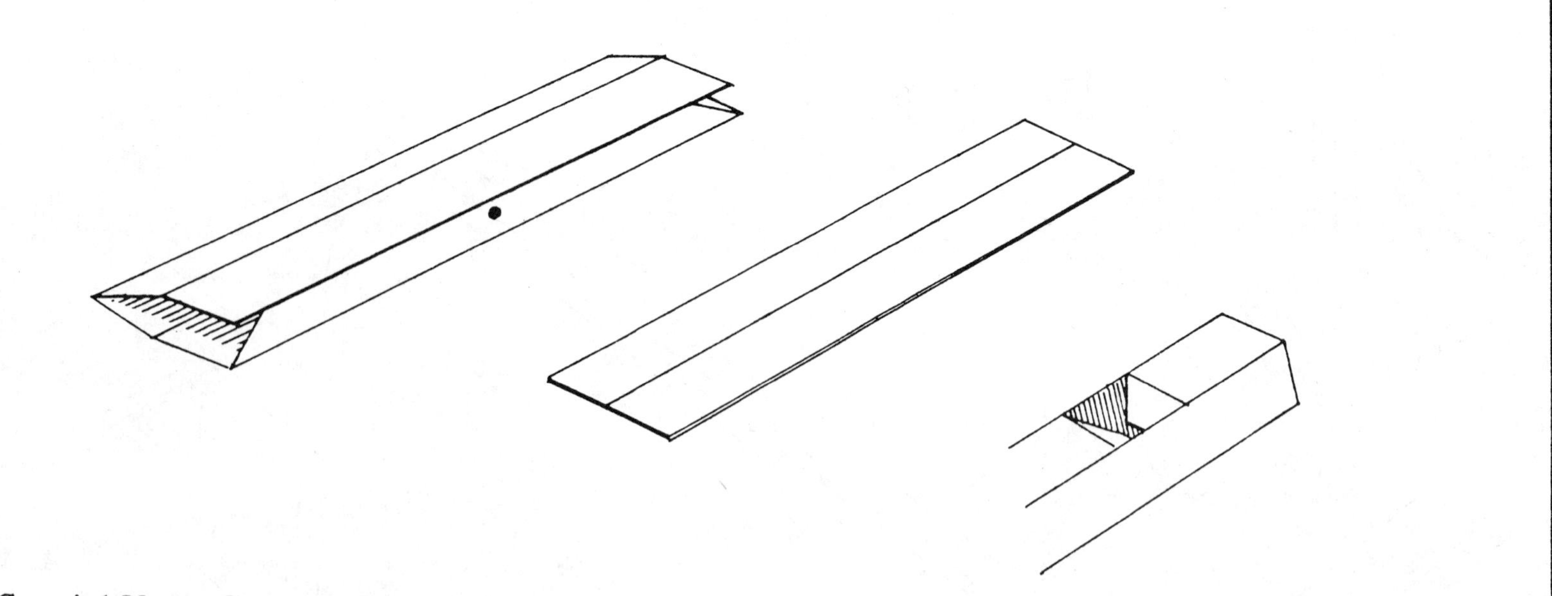

Special Note: Construction of Timbers

We have illustrated here the best method of constructing timbers. Cut and score each piece and be sure that you cut the small flaps to make the openings as well. Then fold each timber so that two of the sides plus the glue-tab, which is indicated with a dot, are positioned under the other two sides. Apply glue to the glue-tab surface and then smooth the glue out with the straight edge of a scrap of cardboard. Strips for smoothing can be made from unused pieces of background on each page. While the glue is wet, press down firmly on top of the side that meets the glue-tab. Hold until it's dry. Squeeze the outside edges: this should pop open the piece to make a four-sided timber. To open the hole on the surface that receives another timber, press down the two flaps and insert the appropriate timber. When the timbers are finally constructed and you're ready to put them together, the fit will be tight enough to hold them in place without glue.

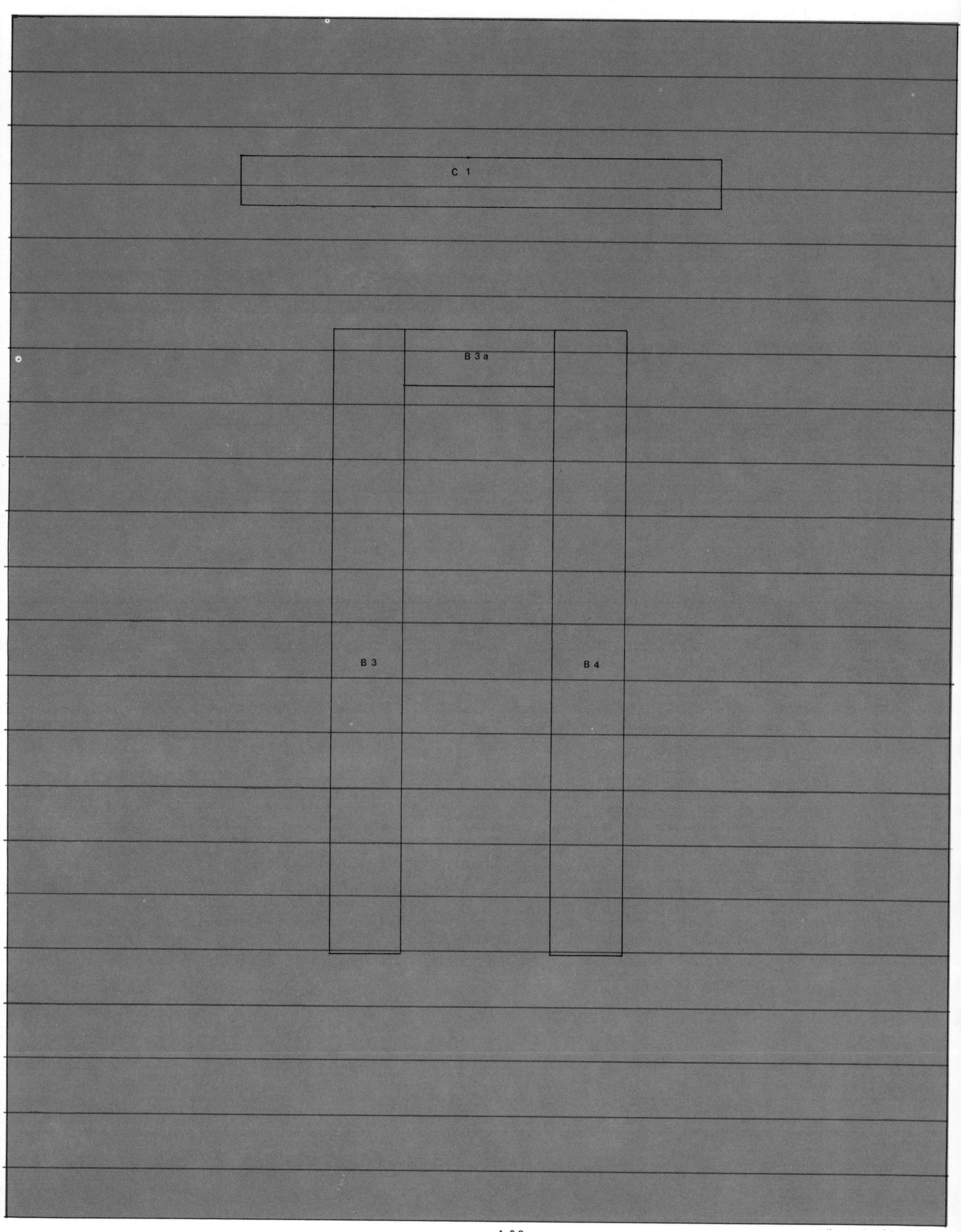
C 1
B 3 a
B 3
B 4

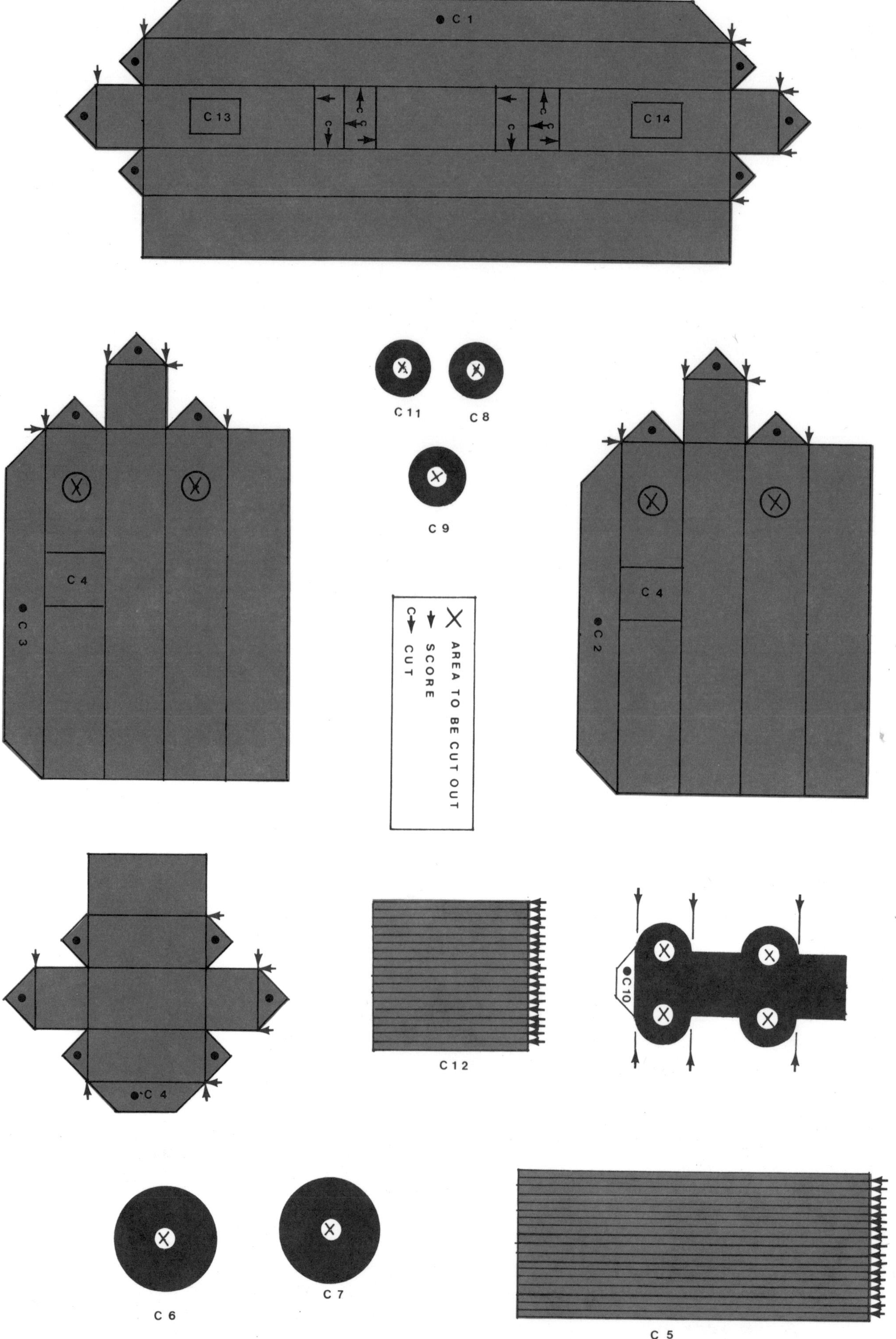

C 1
C 13
C 14
C 11
C 8
C 9
C 3
C 4
C 2
C 4
AREA TO BE CUT OUT
SCORE
CUT
C 4
C 12
C 10
C 6
C 7
C 5

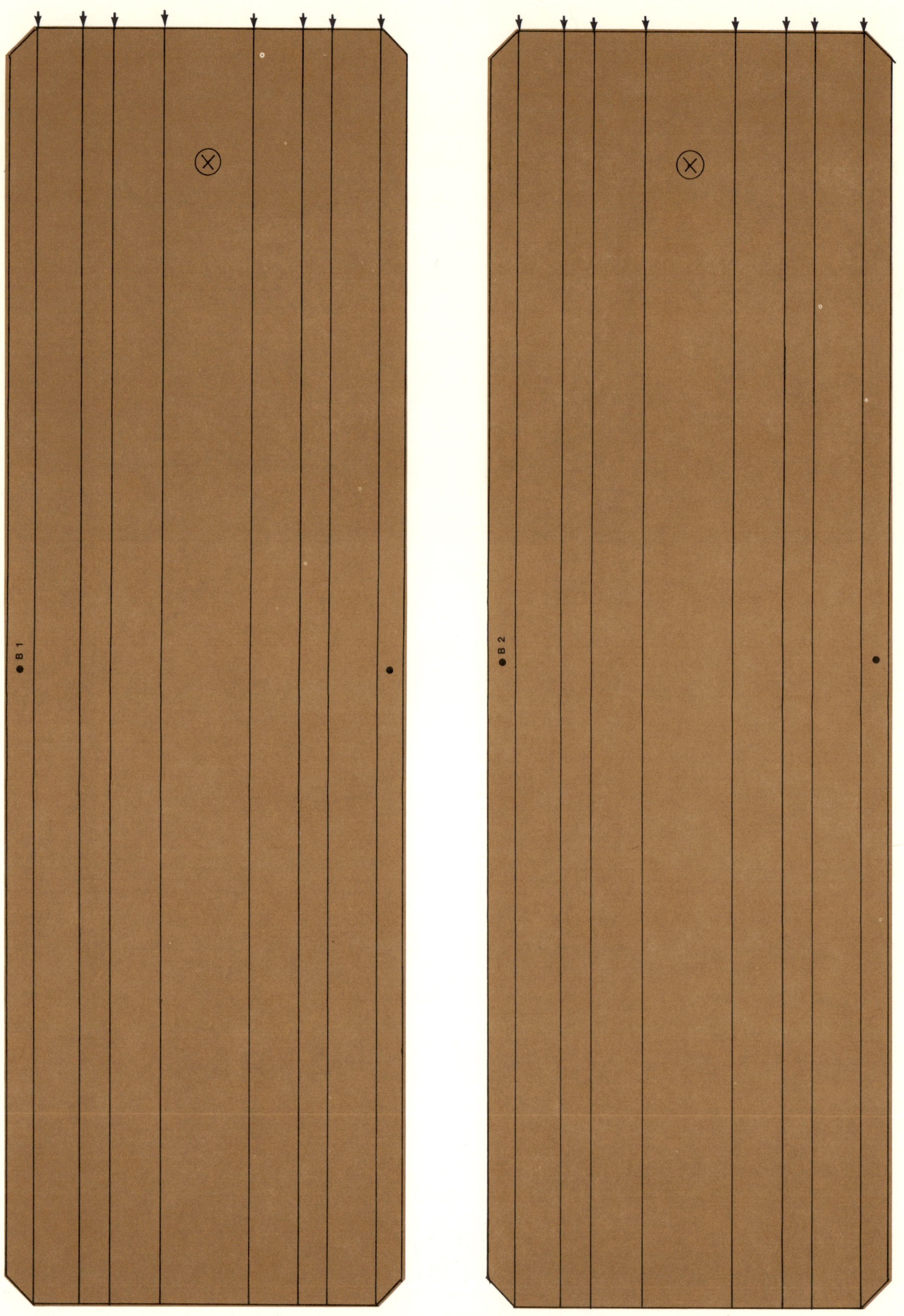
B 1
B 2

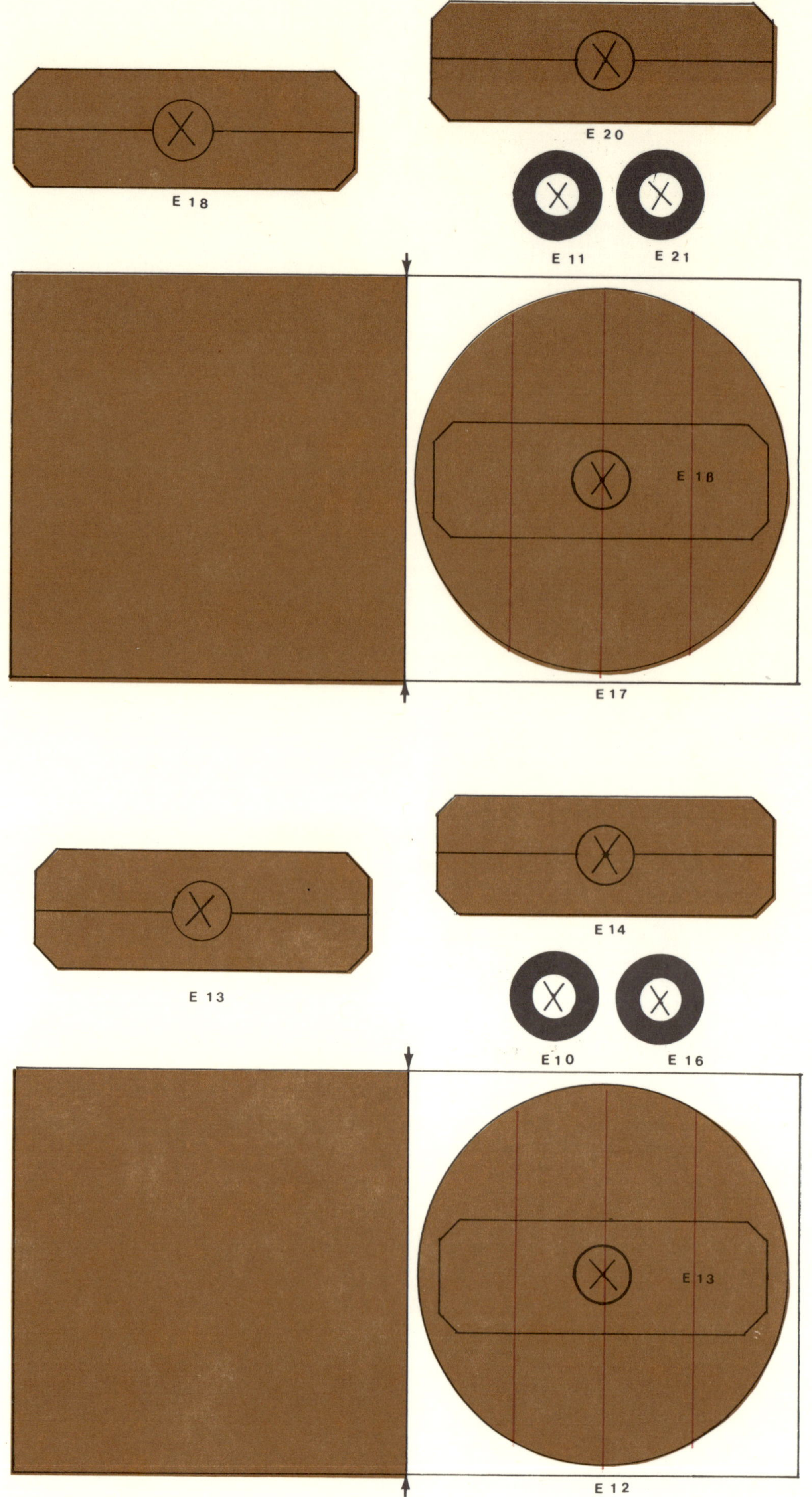

E 15

E 19

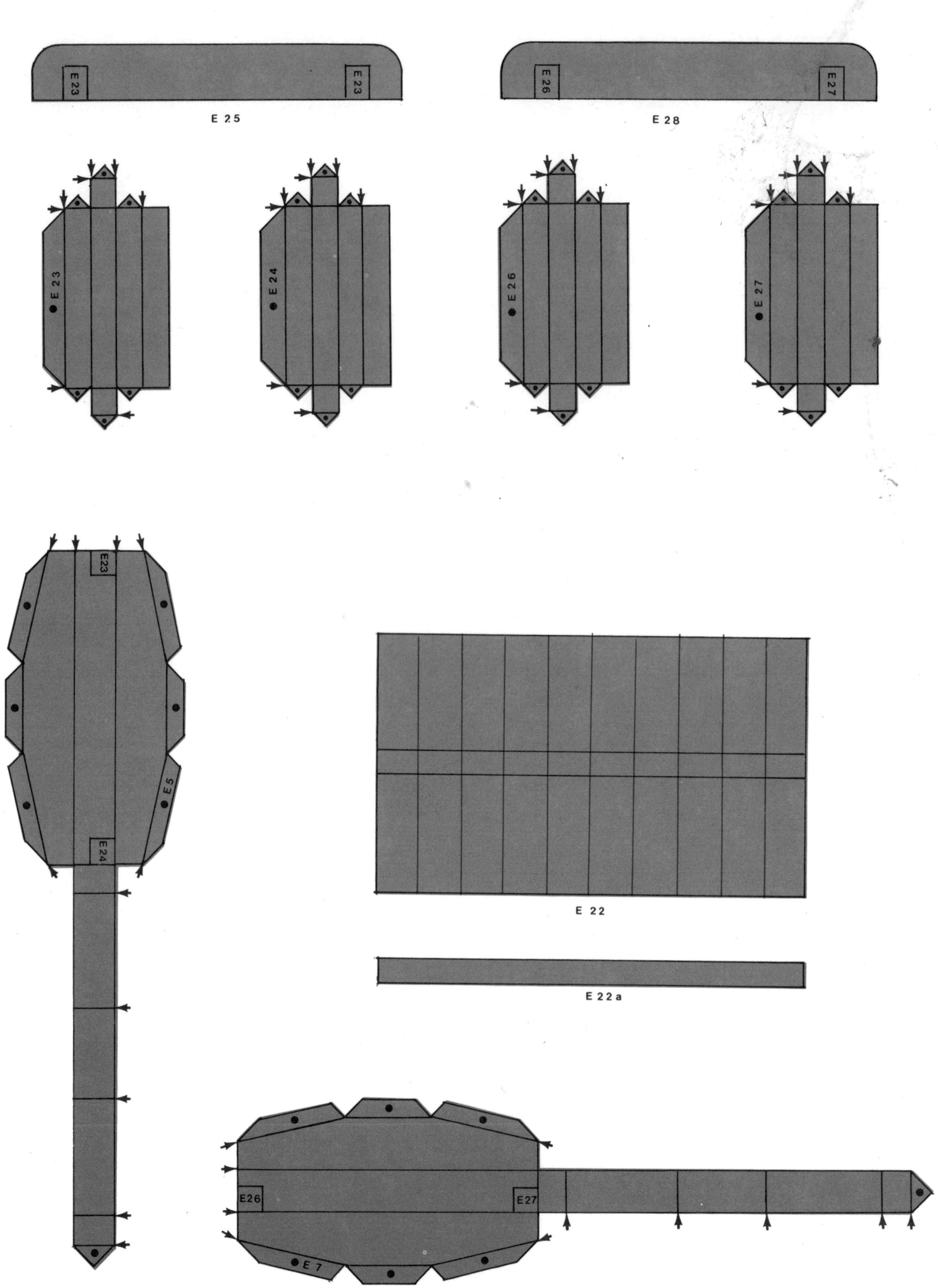
E23
E23
E 25
E26
E27
E 28
E 23
E 24
E 26
E 27
E23
E5
E24
E 22
E 22a
E26
E27
E 7

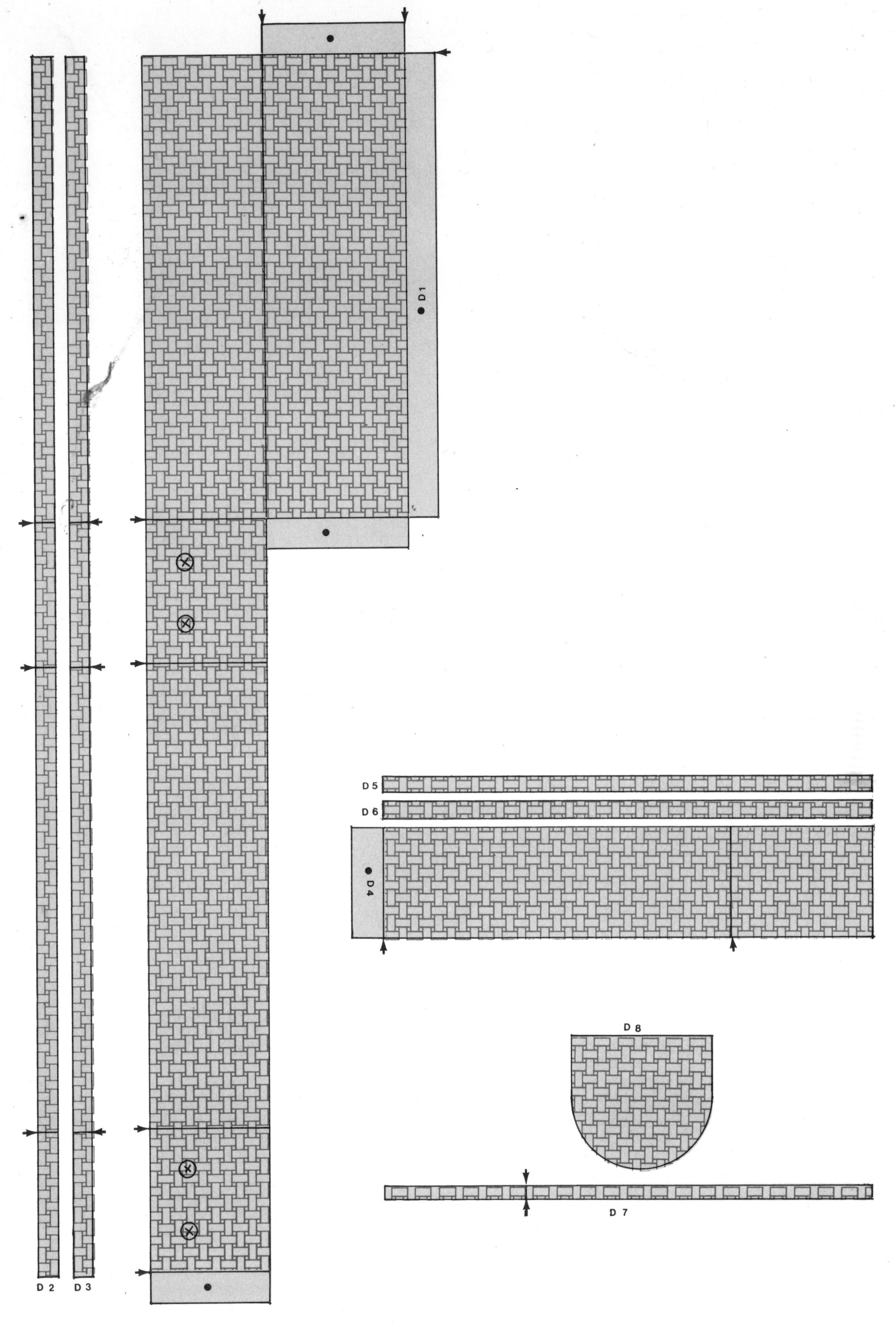
D1
D2
D3
D4
D5
D6
D7
D8

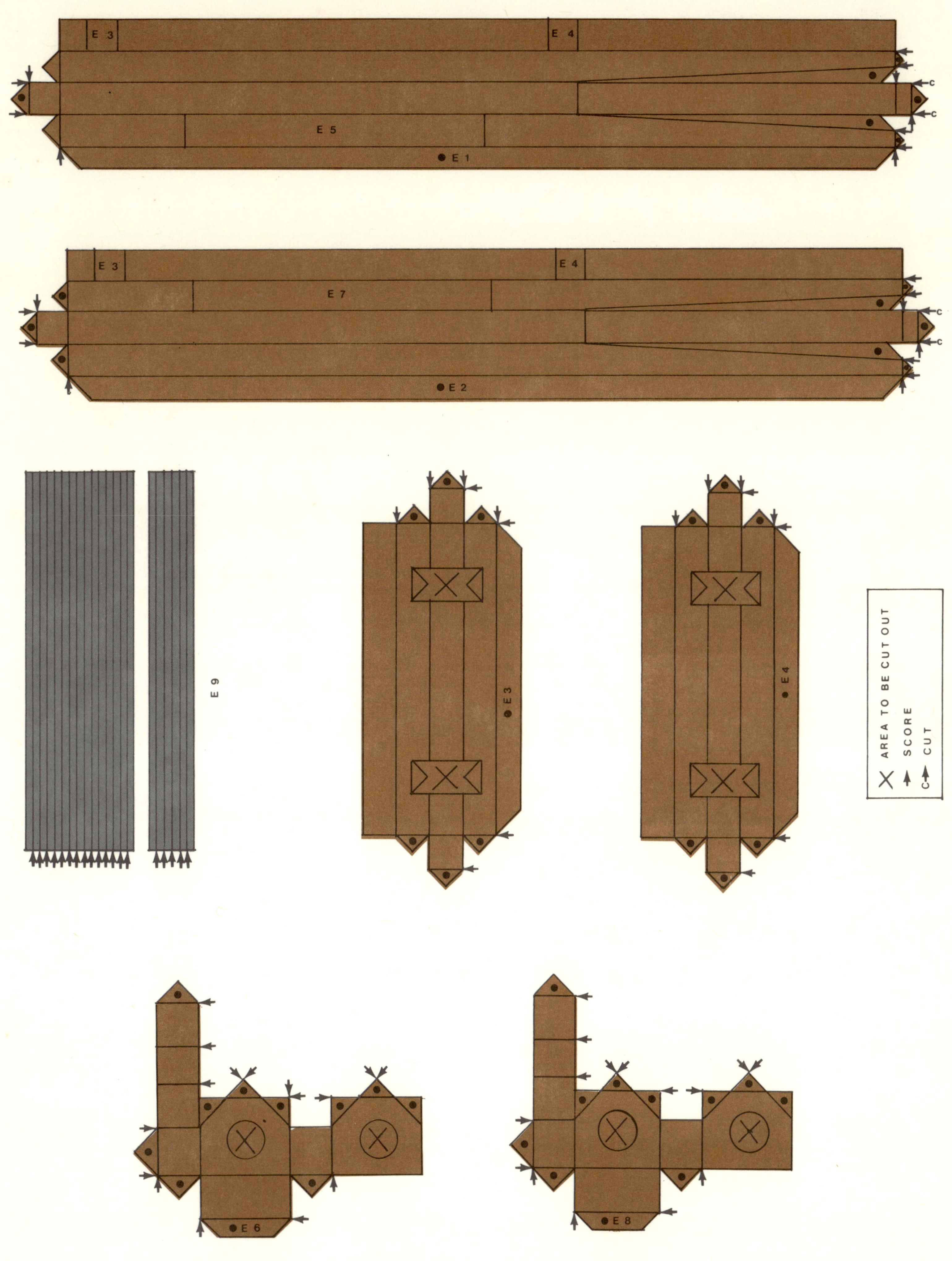
E 3
E 4
E 5
E 1
E 3
E 4
E 7
E 2
C
C
E 9
E 3
E 4
E 6
E 8
AREA TO BE CUT OUT
SCORE
CUT

B 22
B 9
B 10
B 5
B 6
B 21
B 17
B 18
B 20
B 19
B 8
B 7
B 16

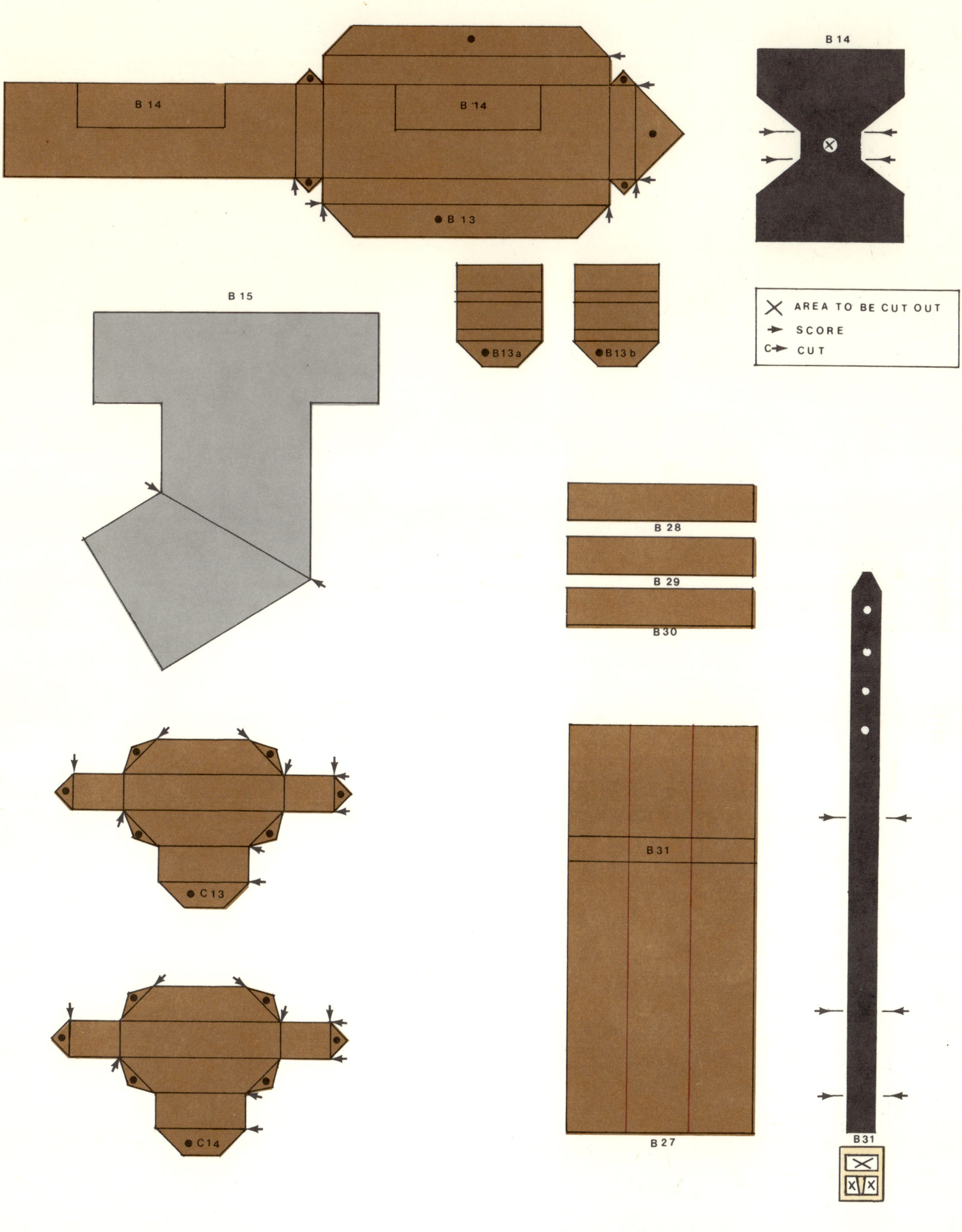
B 14
B 14
B 13
B 14
B13a
B13b
AREA TO BE CUT OUT
SCORE
CUT
B 15
B 28
B 29
B30
B31
B 27
B31
C13
C14

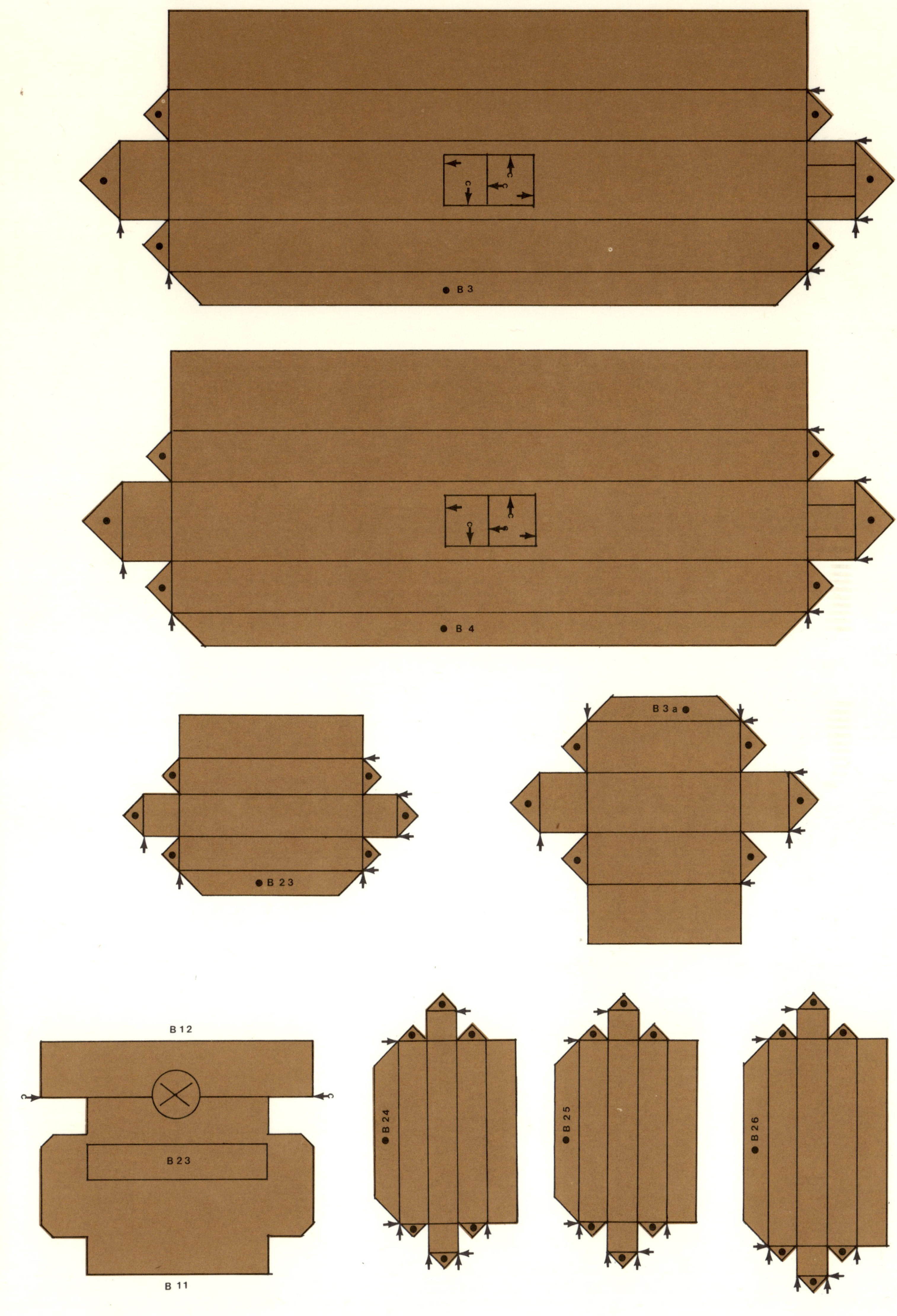
B 3
B 4
B 3 a
B 23
B 12
B 23
B 11
B 24
B 25
B 26
A 29

A 22

A 23

AREA TO BE CUT OUT
SCORE
CUT

A 39

A 30

A 31 A 32 A 33 A 34 A 35 A 36 A 37 A 38

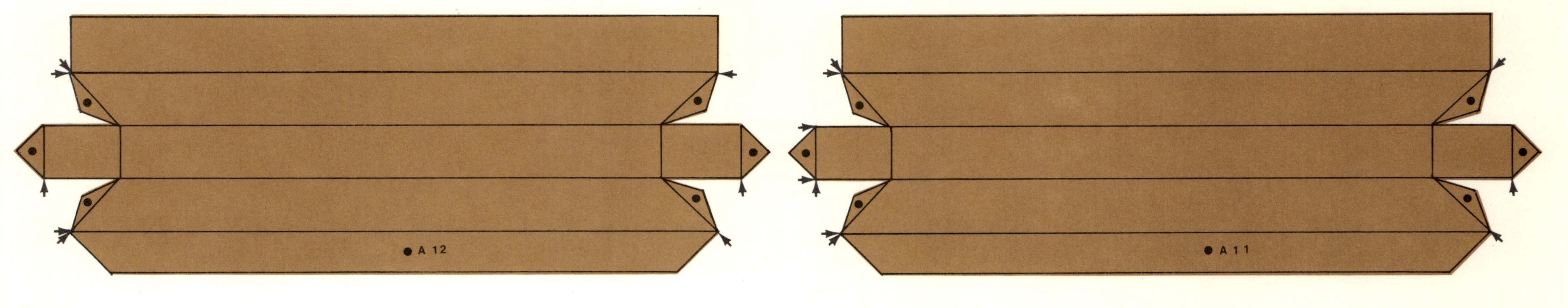
A 12
A 11
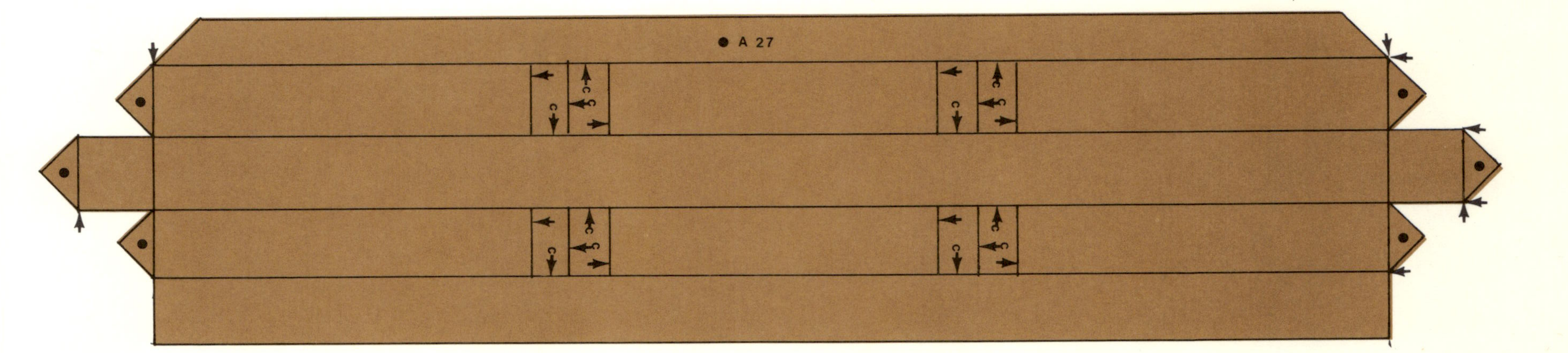
A 27

A 26

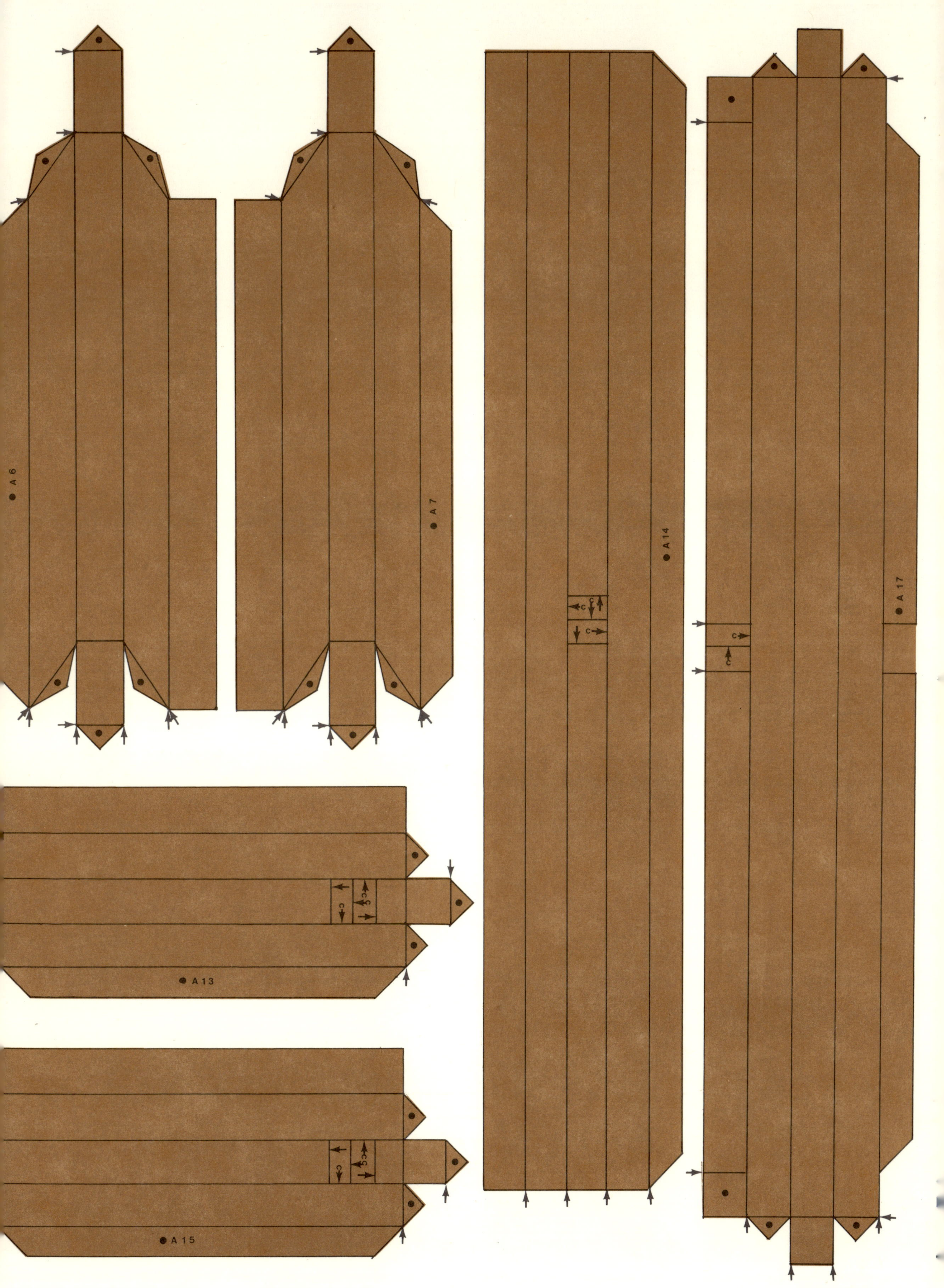
A 6
A 7
A 14
A 17
A 13
A 15

ERRATUM: Pieces A11, A12, A23 and A24 inside this book are incorrect. Please substitute the pieces on this page for them.

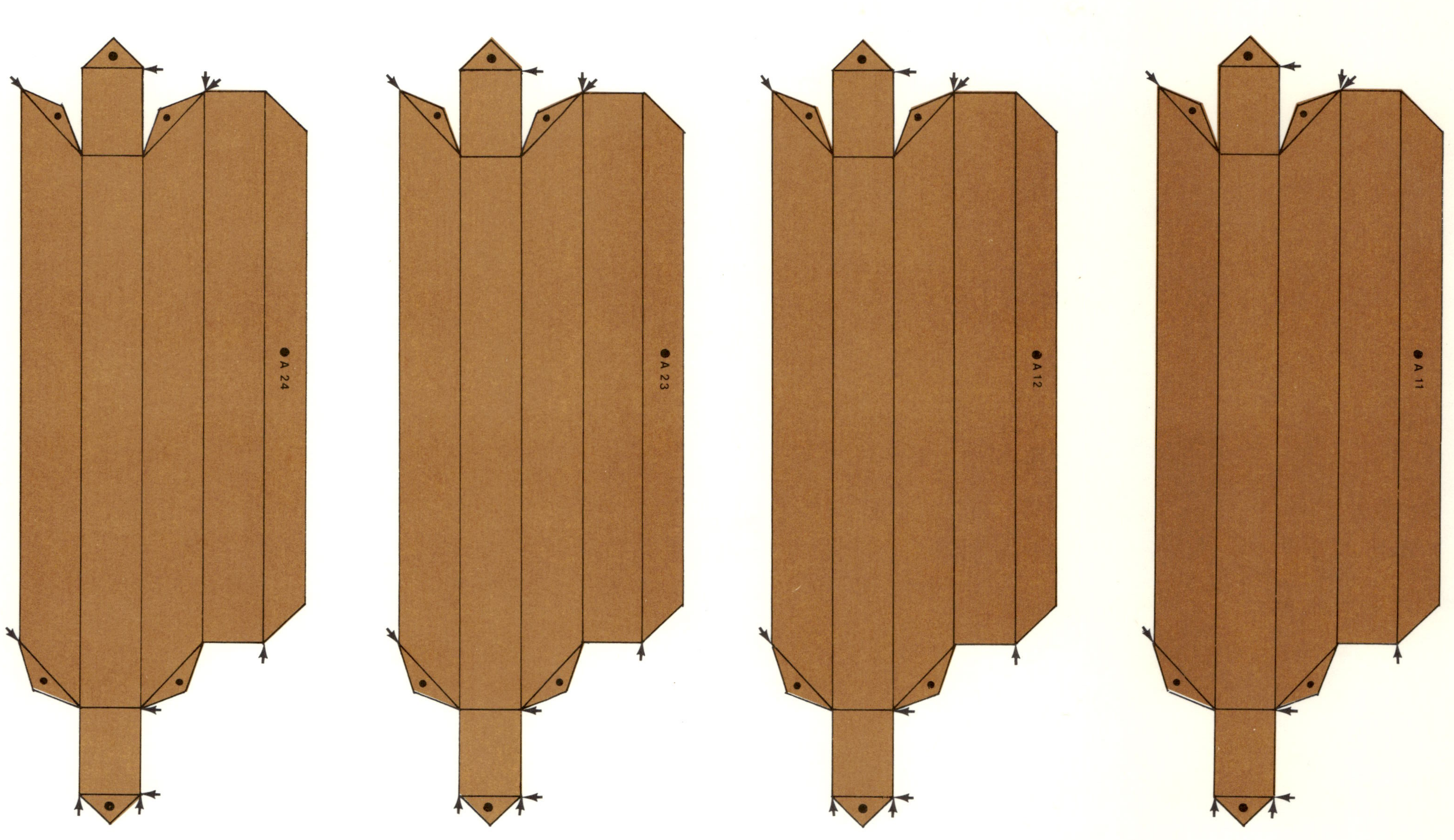

First published 1972
First published in the USA in 1973

ISBN 0 200 71745 6 (Trade)
ISBN 0 200 71887 8 (GB) (USA only)
L.C.C.C. NO. 74-38427

LONDON
Abelard-Schuman
Limited
158 Buckingham Palace Road
SW1W 9TR

NEW YORK
Abelard-Schuman
Limited
257 Park Avenue South
New York 10010

Printed in Great Britain by Gilmour & Dean Limited,
Hamilton and London.

A Sultana for the Sultan
Martin Baker
Abelard-Schuman

The mighty Sultan Saladin, Lord of the East and ruler of the Holy Land, had a great sadness in his heart. It was this: in all his empire he could not find a sultana sweet enough for his taste.

He commanded his wisest men and bravest soldiers to search to the North, South, East and West of his lands for such a sultana. But, after months of fruitless searching, all they could show him were sultanas that looked so sour that the sad Sultan flew into a temper.

His palace became crowded with people bringing him sultanas chosen for their sweetness, but as the Sultan tasted each one he pronounced that it tasted even more sour than the one he had tasted before.

The gloomy Sultan retired to his rooms and brooded on the fact that there was not a sultana sweet enough for his taste to be had in all his lands. His servants were beaten when they brought him food, and they were beaten when they did not bring him food. His wise men were beaten when they brought him wisdom, and they were beaten when they did not bring him wisdom. His soldiers were beaten too, but only because they made too much noise when they got drunk.

One day the wise men saw storm clouds in the West, and flocks of birds flying to the East. They prophesied that a great army was sailing toward the Holy Land to do battle. The Sultan grew very angry. "I will not fight without first finding a sultana that is sweet enough for my taste!" he said.

The wise men departed trembling with fear. The soldiers sharpened their swords and polished their helmets. When the foreign army sailed into port, messengers were sent to ask their King not to start fighting until further notice.

The King's army pitched their tents outside the Sultan's palace and were taken gifts of spice cakes and coffee. They were very happy at this turn of events, for their King did not really want to fight at all: he just wanted to get away from his nagging wife.

The days passed and still the sweet sultana had not been found. The Sultan invited the King to his palace, where they played many games to pass the time. Best of all the King enjoyed Silent Wrestling, which is like wrestling, except that the wrestlers do not touch each other. They also played Pin the Tail on the Stallion, Push the Marble, Pinch the Pasha, Crescents and Crosses and What's the Time Mr. Camel. The Sultan completely forgot his sadness at the jollity of it all, and the King quite forgot that he had come to do battle.

One day, after a hectic game of Pin the Tail on the Stallion, the King received a letter from his wife. She wrote angrily that since he had not sent any news she was coming herself to see how the battle progressed. The King's nose went bright red, and he started to run around in circles. "What will I do?" he cried. "I could not possibly fight you after your kind hospitality."

The Sultan thought for a moment and then replied, "Your wife expects to see a battle when she arrives, therefore, my dear King, we will pretend to fight!" The King thought this an excellent idea and together they sat down to plan the war.

When the Queen sailed into harbour she saw the most terrible fighting going on. There on the quayside she saw the Sultan striking the King on the head with a huge sword, and the King hitting the Sultan with a wooden club. There were soldiers everywhere, rolling on the grass, jumping from rooftops and making the most fearful noises.

Then the Sultan, with a warlike cry, threw the King over his shoulder, and tossed him into the sea. The Queen was so distressed that she jumped into the sea after her husband crying, "Oh my poor Willibald, you'll catch a death of cold."

And the Sultan and all the soldiers laughed behind their hands, because really they were having a wonderful time.

When the Queen and the King had been fished from the sea, the Sultan declared that war was over for the day, and invited them to dine with him. He gave a delicious dinner. His cooks prepared mouth-watering delicacies like Turkey in Persian Pie, Crocodile in Red Sea Sauce and Chicken à la Sultan. Meanwhile, in the fields outside the Sultan's palace, the soldiers of both armies sat round camp fires and told each other hilarious jokes.

Mellowed by the rich food and wine, the Sultan confided to the Queen the sadness in his heart—that he could not find, in all his lands, a sultana sweet enough for his taste.

"My dear Sultan!" exclaimed the Queen boastfully. "At my palace I grow the sweetest sultanas in the world. I will return home and bring you enough to make your heart content!"

The Sultan was overjoyed at her offer, and begged her to set sail the very next day.

After seventeen days and nights the Queen returned in a right regal temper. She had found not a single sultana at home, for the King had eaten them all before sailing to do battle.

But the Sultan was undismayed. He was gazing at the most beautiful young lady he had ever seen. She was the daughter of the King and Queen, the Princess Melissende, who had accompanied her mother on the return trip to the Sultan's land. The Sultan was entranced by her loveliness. "Her beauty is more sweet than any sultana. It is she who will banish the sadness from my heart."

Sultan Saladin and Princess Melissende fell in love immediately and were married the very next day. After a week of celebration and festivities the King and Queen sailed home. The Queen was so delighted at making such a good match for her daughter that she forgave the King for eating all her sultanas.

The Sultan and his new wife lived happily ever after. And to this day, the wife of every Sultan is called a Sultana, because she is the only one sweet enough for his taste.